LADYBUG, LADYBUG, FLY AWAY HOME

By Judy Hawes / Illustrated by Ed Emberley

Thomas Y. Crowell Company, New York

"Ladybug, ladybug, fly away home!"
Why do we say that?
We shoo flies, and we slap at mosquitoes, but we are
gentle with ladybugs. Why? Let's see if we can find
out.

But first, let's take a close look at a ladybug.

A ladybug has three parts:

1. The body is the largest part. It is covered by a round shell. The shell is usually red with black dots.
2. The small shield is in front of the body. It is frequently black, with yellow or white markings.
3. The tiny head is partly hidden by the shield. It, too, is usually black, with white markings.

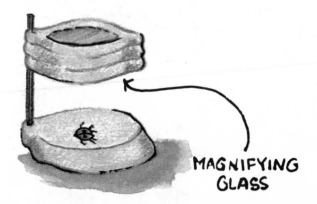

MAGNIFYING
GLASS

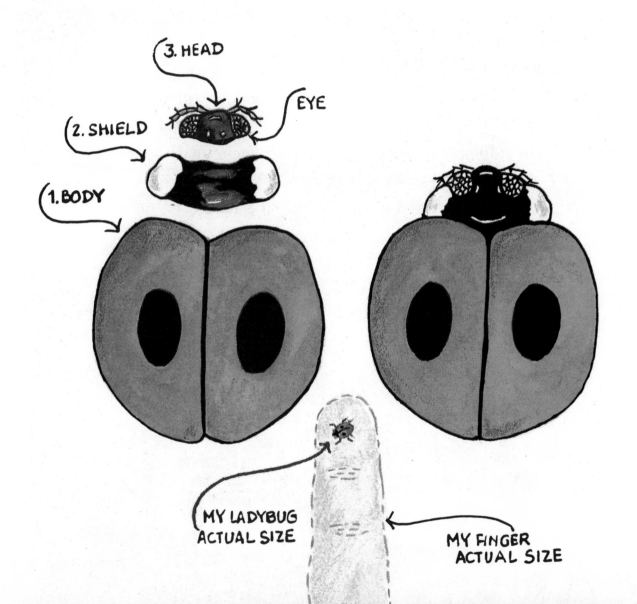

3. HEAD

EYE

2. SHIELD

1. BODY

MY LADYBUG
ACTUAL SIZE

MY FINGER
ACTUAL SIZE

3

Let's look at a ladybug through a magnifying glass.
Can you see the stout feelers on the head, next to
its big bulging eyes? The feelers are for smelling and
touching food. Can you see the jaws? They are very
strong. Next to them, you can see a pair of short,
bent "palps." The palps are for tasting food.

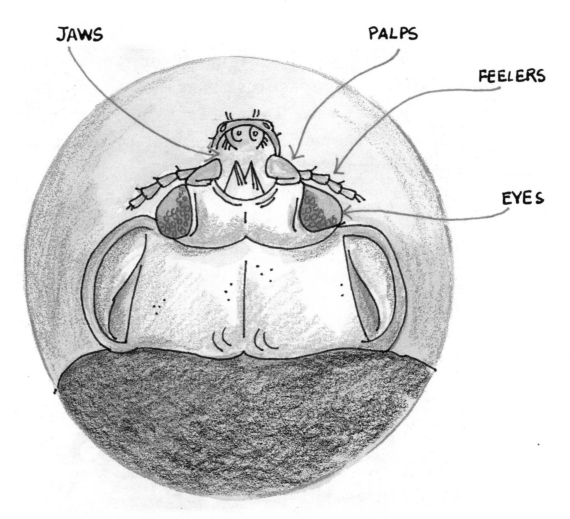

JAWS

PALPS

FEELERS

EYES

UNDERSIDE OF LADYBUG — MUCH MAGNIFIED

5

Watch a ladybug closely as it starts to fly. The back separates down the center into two wing covers. The ladybug holds up the covers and then unfolds a pair of big, filmy wings. The wings go so fast, it is hard to see anything but a blur. The wing covers do not move during flight.

When a ladybug lands, it looks rather untidy. The wings stick out beyond the wing covers. Watch the ladybug fold its wings and tuck them neatly under the wing covers.

A ladybug has six short legs. Two are on the shield, and four on the body. At the end of each leg is a small, sharp claw. Above each claw is a sticky pad. These sticky pads help ladybugs walk up smooth, slippery walls and windowpanes.

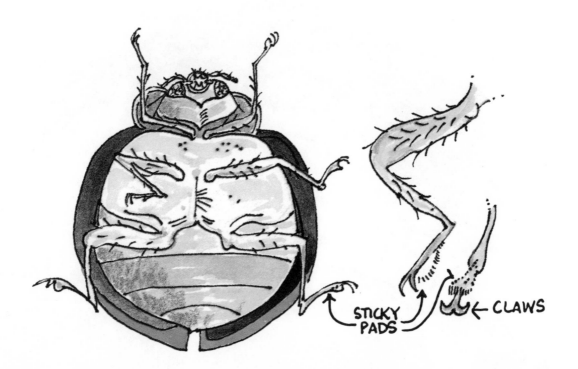

STICKY
PADS

← CLAWS

Ladybugs clean themselves with their legs. Watch a ladybug scrub its face with its front legs. It nibbles the dust off one front leg, then the other. It cleans the middle and back pairs of legs by rubbing them against each other. It scrapes its wings clean between the wing covers and the back feet.

11

Ladybugs are supposed to bring you good luck. Let a ladybug walk across your hand. Ladybugs do not bite; maybe that is part of the luck.

The name "ladybug" was given them long ago in honor of the Virgin Mary, who was called Our Lady. Some people call them "ladybirds" or "lady beetles." The name does *not* mean that all ladybugs are females. There are just as many male ladybugs as female ladybugs.

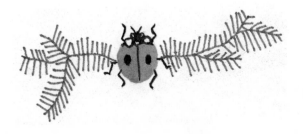

The old familiar verse continues: "Ladybug, ladybug, fly away home, your house is on fire, your children will burn." What is that all about?

14

Long ago when farmers cleaned up their gardens in the fall, they burned the dead leaves of their vines. Ladybugs had lived on these vines all summer because that is where they found their favorite food —a tiny aphid. The aphids sucked the juice of the leaves, slowly killing the vines. The ladybugs ate the aphids and so saved the vines. Not only fully grown ladybugs, but also their "children" lived on the vines. The farmers' fires scared them all away. Probably most of the children were burned as they cannot fly.

17

In cold weather ladybugs crawl into cracks, under leaves and stones, into pine cones, and under haystacks. They sleep until spring. Some even spend the winter in our houses, especially old houses where they can hide in cracks in the woodwork.

Farmers used to believe it was good luck to have ladybugs winter in their houses. It was said to be a sign of good weather and good crops to come. The farmer's daughter believed that if a ladybug walked across her hand, it meant she would be married within the year. The farmer's wife believed that ladybugs cured toothache, colic, and measles!

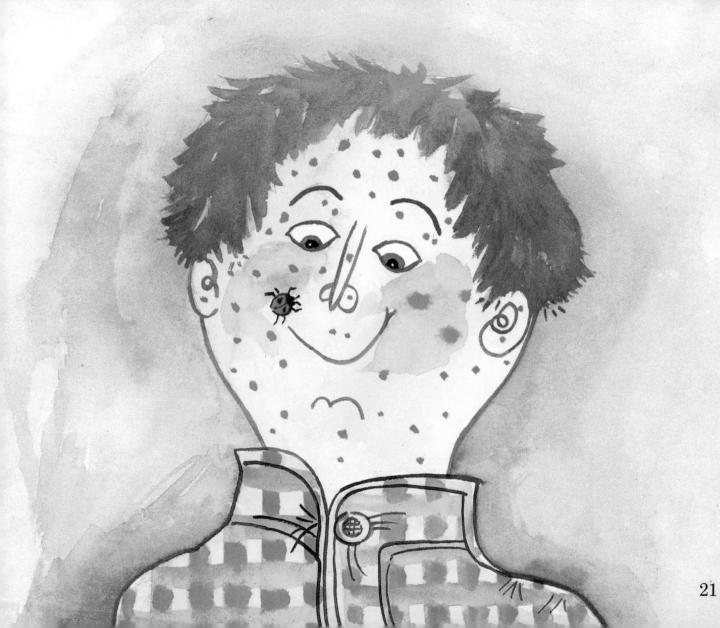

Ladybugs, or ladybirds, are beetles with enormous appetites. Almost all ladybugs eat only harmful insects. A dozen ladybugs can save a fruit tree from ruin by insect pests. No wonder people like ladybugs.

APHIDS

23

Fruit growers in California have had good reason to be thankful for ladybugs. Just a few hundred ladybugs saved all the orange trees in the state of California.

Back in the 1880's the orange trees were attacked by a peculiar insect. It was called the cottony-cushion scale. This insect pest had come into the country on a cargo ship from Australia.

The cottony-cushion scale was known as a pest in Australia, but it did not do as much damage there as it did in California. This was because there were ladybugs in Australia that ate their weight in cottony-cushion scale every day. These ladybugs

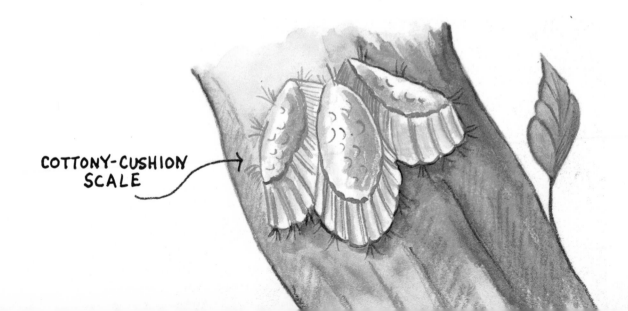

COTTONY-CUSHION
SCALE

kept the pest under control. Five hundred ladybugs were sent to California. They feasted on the cottony-cushion scale in the dying trees. The ladybugs ate and ate. They had children, and then grandchildren. They all ate great quantities of cottony-cushion scale. Within two years the orange trees were saved.

Ladybugs are still used today to control scale insects.

AUSTRALIAN LADYBUG
{RED & BLACK}

Ladybugs live in almost every part of the world. Of the four thousand different kinds, about three hundred and fifty are found in North America. Their colors are red or yellow with black dots, black with red or yellow dots, or plain black. The most common type is red with two black dots. You may see many others with seven or eleven dots.

CONVERGENT
LADYBUG

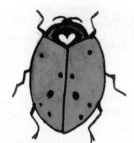

THE AUSTRALIAN
LADYBUG

TWO-SPOTTED
LADYBUG

NINE-SPOTTED
LADYBUG

Ladybugs defend themselves from their enemies in two curious ways. When they are frightened, they topple onto the ground, and pretend to be dead. If they are attacked, they repel the enemy with a bad smell. Ladybugs are able to force an evil-smelling, yellow liquid out through their leg joints.

The next time you find a ladybug, put it to work near
your favorite garden plants. As you let it go, you'll
surely say, "Ladybug, ladybug, fly away home."
And this time you'll know what you are talking about.

ABOUT THE AUTHOR

Mrs. Hawes, mother of four, has worked with children as a teacher and as a leader in scouting and Sunday school. For the past ten years she has taught various kinds of special education classes in the public schools. A native of Forest Hills, New York, she was graduated from Vassar College. Mrs. Hawes and her husband are residents of Glen Rock, New Jersey, where they participate in many community activities.

She is the author of eight other titles in the Let's-Read-and-Find-Out science series, among them *Bees and Beelines, Fireflies in the Night, and Watch Honeybees with Me.*

ABOUT THE ARTIST

Although his days are usually filled with writing and illustrating, Ed Emberley still finds time for his favorite hobbies. He can often be found at his own hand press, printing limited editions of children's books. Mr. Emberley also experiments with toy making and pursues his studies of Americana.

Ed Emberley received a B.F.A. degree in illustration from the Massachusetts School of Art in Boston. He lives in Ipswich, Massachusetts.